Brave Bird

Patricia Sauer

BookLeaf Publishing

India | USA | UK

Presentation by *BookLeaf Publishing*

Web: www.bookleafpub.com

E-mail: info@bookleafpub.com

ISBN: 9789360942519

First edition 2024

This book of poetry is dedicated to my husband, Scott, who has lived these experiences first hand and who holds my hand everyday.

This book is also dedicated to my boys, Devin and Jonah. Remember always that I love you.

ACKNOWLEDGEMENT

This world is a much better place with the Reflex Sympathetic Dystrophy Syndrome Association (RSDSA) in it. They have been a place for me to look to in order to find research, support, and general information about CRPS. Your work is invaluable to those of us fighting for our lives and to the caretakers who are in the trenches with us.

To the CRPS Warriors, your fight is my fight and you inspire me to keep going, and keep fighting.

To my family and friends who took the time, from the beginning, to do research, ask questions and offer help whenever possible. I appreciate you and am blessed to have you in my life.

To my husband Scott, and my boys, Devin and Jonah. Thank you for loving me through this mess. It was not the life we chose, but it's the one we make the most of. Thank you for fighting with me and rooting for me when times are truly tough. You have quietly stood by and held my hand and wiped my tears on more than one occasion and I am so grateful. I'm not sure I could continue to fight if I didn't have you.

PREFACE

This book of poetry is a compilation of my
thoughts and feelings as I've experienced Type I
Chronic Regional Pain Syndrome (CRPS). I was
diagnosed in 2018 and have soldiered through,
fighting an uphill battle. I, like many Chronic
Pain Warriors, live in the in-between: trying to
live the life we used to know and the one we
have come to deal with. I was compelled to
write this book of poetry in order for my words,
and the words of others in the same battle, to be
heard. I want other Warriors to know that they
are not alone, and to find hope in each day.

To find out more about Chronic Regional Pain
Syndrome, you can visit: www.rsdsa.org

Twenty-One Steps from the Gates of Hell

He stared back at me,
Pleading, wanting, enticing.
Grinning back in his predatory welcome.
Is this my penance?
Is this my purgatory?

You will not survive out there.
You will come in.

I stand on coal covered feet.
Blackness up to my knee.
The fire is seeping slowly,
Electrifying the fiber optics of my soul.

It is what he wants,
But I still stand twenty one steps from the gates
of hell.

And So It Began

Unaware ....
A cold gray day unsuspecting that such a place
exists.
Walking and making great plans for the days and
weeks ahead.
Looking forward to opportunity, success and
happiness.
It began....
Unwitting of a place such as the one I will arrive
at very soon.
Only a chosen few are allowed entry to
This Place and this Never-ending Season that
bears the sign:
No Return

The Blue Bench

There is a blue bench that beckons me,
Among the forest of dancing trees.
I know who sits with ebony hair,
His hand lays gently upon that faithful chair.
Look. Listen. See.
There is peace in this seat right next to me.

Brain Fog

Tofsay,
(Today,)

It's in the other room.
(I don't know why I walked into this room.)

Blurred vision.
Dissociation of the present.

What words?
(I cannot find my words.)

Why scribe?
(I cannot describe what I'm looking for.)

How to spell?
(I cannot spell my meaning.)

The Tide

There is a line of us that stands along the ocean's shore.
We feel the ebb and flow, a tug of war.
Its Sirens decide between war and peace.
Some lean closer to the cradle of peace.
Others battle the war of pain.
They take a stand over and over again.
Fear bubbles in and quietly rolls.
I feel its current stinging between my toes.
Mother, Daughter, Sister and Friend.
Will this struggle ever end?
They will never run away and hide,
Even if they're all so close to the deep dark tide.

Battery Operated

I used to run, walk, jump, climb, laugh and smile
all on my own.
Now...
I don't run, walk, jump or climb.
My laugh and my smile?
Not fake.
Just battery operated.

"Gift of Life"

The weight of the world feels so burdensome.
Those that have practiced lifting it,
Feel its fleshy weight.
Felo-de-se?
Or, freedom and liberty?

In this seventh circle,
Isolation is full of broken branches.
It is an eternal pain,
That burns and lays bare the "gift of life."

#lessonlearned

I woke up feeling rejuvenated,
This is the first time in many days.
My To-Do List, ready to be exterminated,
preparing to be razed.

I dust and mop,
And sweep and shop.
I smile as I go.
My battery is running at optimal strength,
And shows that my spoons are full.

So, I drive and sing,
And walk with a spring.
My feet have nothing to fear.

But, upon returning,
My battery slowing and churning,
My brain has just confirmed.

Tomorrow, I'll say,
While in bed where I'll lay.
"I am definitely running on empty."
#lessonlearned

Blessings

It's hard to find blessings in between the popcorn
garland and tinsel.
Gazing deeper in and through the stained glass
colored lights and nostalgia,
It peeks and pulses its shining star;
My lighthouse.
A reminder of my full heart and the Loves of my
life.
These are my blessings each and every day.

Lonely Mitten

I am a lonely Mitten,
 in the foggy mist.
I must have been the only one,
 on Santa's Naughty List.

Snow Geese

The winter's chill has set in.
Thousands of Snow Geese appear above as a
lazy carpet.
Soaring and swirling overhead, but going
nowhere,
The deafening flock, honking, and making their
presence known.

Watching in awe and fascination a skulk of foxes
prowl this gaggle.
Together, this sly and cunning crew of orange
work together to balance the welfare of these
aviaries.

Flapping their outspread wings, it seems a
complicated and ongoing task is ahead.
Ever vigilant, the bodies heave, wrench and
steam as they rip and pull at the roots they
hunger for.

Will the fox, on the edge of its hiding place,
pounce and devour the poor souls right where
they toll,
Or will he continue studying with curiosity
while his adversary cranes and wrenches his
black neck?

Wild Ice Skating

In a tiny crack between the snow-capped
mountains,
There is a valley so very far away.
Hidden, is an idyllic escape,
where a back-country pond lay.

A shadow of black underneath shimmering blue
ice,
holds two boots of patent white.
A one-legged blade, smiles a twirling
figure-eight
that just might take an ephemeral flight.

At complete mercy to nature,
And praying not to fall,
She is mesmerized by the dank underwater
shoal.

Deep gashes and scars begin marring this
glassy, transparent rink,
The edges in white, hitting the jackpot like a
hunter's instincts,
Where fight or flight could be hi-jinked.

She wonders, for a moment, on this placid lake,
Fearing the frozen frog's bubbles
which loom dark and psychedelic.
Nevertheless, with her arms outstretched, she
continues her pirouettes.

She breathes in the cold,
Hidden along an old snow-dusted road,
And revels in her wild ice skating.

It's All a Facade

Just a bunch of broken puzzle pieces,
Underneath a pretty party dress.

Why reveal the truth when no one believes?
It's easier to wear the crown, than to describe
what burns within the edges.

Epic Quest

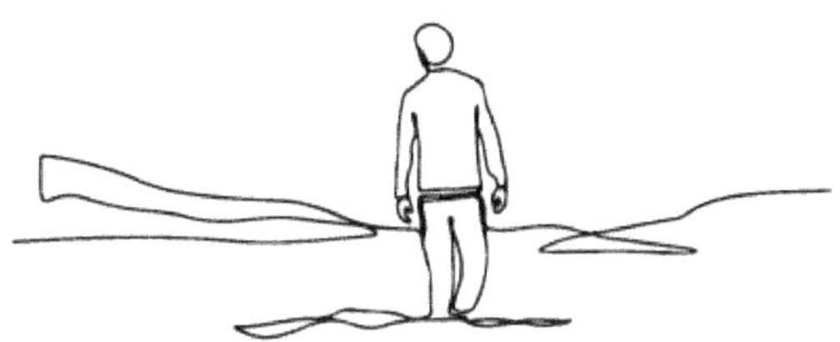

There is no Chariot of Fire for this race.
Only Mercury's winged feet.
This Odyssey stretches for many kilometers,
And he must go alone.
The crowd watches his trepidation and fear of
the unknown.
Where will he go carrying only an end in mind?
His mind....
Conversations with Ego and Id,
Thoughts full of a sulfuric fog.
The epic battles over mountains and seas.
Nearly broken and wandering with a heavy heat
upon his chest,
He trudges through his journey.
His shield in pieces and clothes in tatters, and
even some missing.
I know he battles for my honor, yet I know not
of his whereabouts.
I cannot reach him should a rescue party be
dispatched.

I worry, and yet I wonder,
Will he remember when he gets back?
He trudges through the final leg of his journey,
I see him straining to the finish with eyes in
distant places.
Look at me, remember me.
Does he not see the end?
Is there another battle that has beckoned to him?
Does he know this crusade will never end?

Frosted Windowpane

To survive these fiery nights,
I must remain in a foggy medicated state.
The frosted windowpane, from which I gaze,
Will never thaw.
Sometimes the haze lifts for a moment, and
Life becomes clear through the dripping
condensation.
Unfortunately, this time passes and
I am reunited with the molten handshake of
Pain.
Nearby is my medicinal companion,
And its roughened coating of opaqueness.
It sits with me as I easily relax into its numb
security.
I am shielded from the bombardment for another
day.

Snow

There is so much happiness in the first snow of the season,
A nostalgic distraction from the monotony of every other day.
I can't help but stand outside and let the feathery snowflakes fall onto my upturned face.
A faint touch, that on any other day, would send a mock blow to my brain.
Instead, today, my thoughts are distracted by wondrous memories of winter's past.

A New Year

Staring up at the midnight skies,
I begin to count.
3....2....1....
My wish for the New Year?
Please, not the same year that the groundhog
keeps returning to me.
Instead, a year of Hope, Happiness, Courage,
Strength....
No Pain.
Is it too much to ask for?
I guess wishing never hurts.

Fire

A brain gone rogue that sends fire through my veins.
Bone scans that give every indication of being science fiction,
Except there is no Time Machine in my biography.
Merely a well, that is sparsely lit, with the orange ribbons of vanishing time.

Hope

How am I supposed to
Overcome a disease that
Paralyzes my
Entire nervous system?

Brave Bird

There is a little gray bird who looks worn and
drenched,
Bracing against the cold and blustery weather.
She's digging down deep with her white talons
clenched,
Holding tight, and fluffing her sweater of
feathers.

The howling wind whistles,
The ice; sharply spiked thistles,
The brave Bird, there is not even one flinch.

She bares down and lays in wait,
For the snow to abate,
As she braves this cold and blustery winter.

Old Flame

Walking side-by-side, I reach for your hand.
It's always there; an instinctual clasp;
Without looking.
Like two magnets attracted by a wave of
particles meant to be together.
No name needs to be called; sometimes only a
glance.
It is not out of meekness, but to feel the
thrumming energy of a complete circuit.
Without this union there is merely an unlit match
without a flame.

In the Haze

The misty, translucent fog surrounds the quiet
little inlet.
There on the lake, sits a little red boat
surrounded by the shade of white and gray.
This ghostly blanket drifts over the still water
where only a dark shadow is dawning.
The pine trees on the shoreline, still slumber in
these black-green shadows.
Below, the waterfront is just starting to stretch
out from its slumbering inlet sand.
It seems there should be a fisherman who will
arrive to pull in his tethered keel.
It has drifted out in waves of dreams, but still
awaits its faithful captain.
Look there, dark and deep is the misty quay.
The fog has brought the silent skipper on drifts
of angel wings for another troll around the
waterway.

All Gone

27

All gone is the strangeness of an empty agenda.
No open tabs or workplace sanctions.
No games.
All of that is now trivial to me.
The pursuit of life and meaning are my purpose.

Orb

There the mysterious man stood holding the
mystical orb,
Staring intently into its magical mist.
His free hand the driver of the swirling scherzo,
Manipulating the visions that exist.
It is an exercise to perfect the movement from
which something larger exists.
Is he directing the grand symphonic
composition, or reconciling the dissonance of a
sonata?
Only the conductor knows which strings to
pluck in this emotional to and fro, before its
melodic coda.

The Difference

It was different.
There is no other word.
Like stepping in a puddle;
Being weighed down by the slogging foot.
My eyes glazed over, waiting for the fog to clear.
Trying to relax while being peppered with
questions that my mouth cannot answer,
My brain cannot completely understand.

It was different.
Like touching the skin of someone else,
Yet knowing it is your own.
Your fingers feeling its texture,
Yet your body does not recognize its own touch.

It was different.
Like the kind of madness inducing fear that
brings forth chaos in the mind that it cannot
fathom.

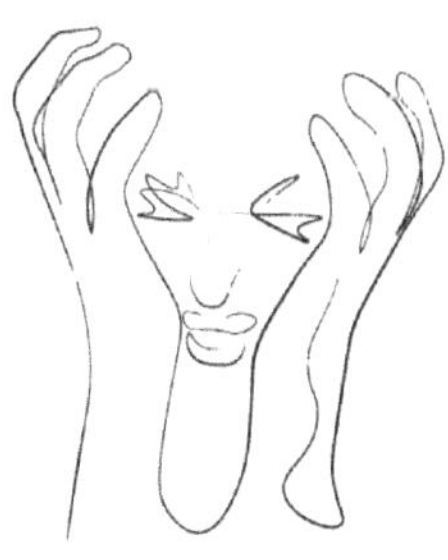

It was different.
Being thrown into an uncontrollable schism with
no knowledge of where you will land.

It was different.
Like pleading for your life before the ground
collapses underneath your feet.
Falling without anything to grasp.

It was different.
Like a prisoner with only the four walls around
you,
The only view you will see for the rest of your
life.
No relief.
No change in scenery.

My life is different now.
Some days, monotony.
Some in fear.
Some unrecognizable.

It is different.
Not being able to conjure up the past,
What it used to be.

It is different.
There is no other word.

Heart of Stone

Time is running out for her.
Not unlike Alice through the looking glass.
She is running in fear of what's behind,
And unknowing of what's ahead.
Her red hair tangled and blanched skin frozen in
fear,
She feels the energy of this touchstone reaching
out,
So close she can sense its being.
Is it testing her pure heart,
Or trying to tempt her to its blackened one?
She cannot look back—does not want to,
But this silicious stoniness has reached inside
And resides now in her soul.
There is no turning back

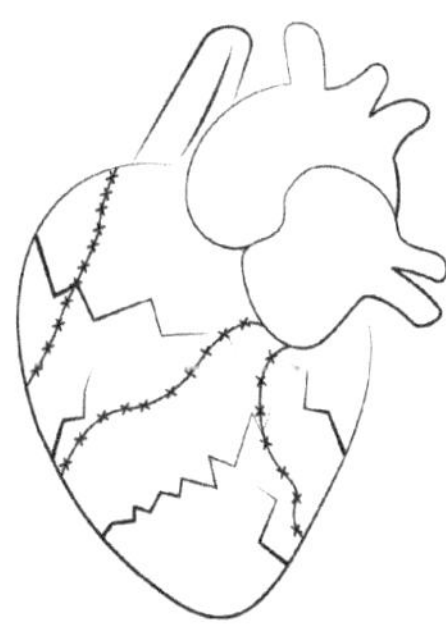

Who

Who is it that's calling from the 10111?
Who is disturbing the beaten down?
Who is this faint voice whose tenor brings the
sun?
Who ignites visions of fun?

A son who becomes the fire for the one who has
come undone.
A man who brings light to the hum of defeat, to
the girl on the run.

Who is it that's calling from the 10111?

In the Land of the Living

Dear Diary,
       Sunday supper is cleared.
A wilted flower with mascara smeared.
I'm finding that Father Time can be unforgiving.
My body aches and my legs are spent.
I know it's essential to enjoy our time on
Thanksgiving.
It is the here and now in which I'm feeling
content.
I'll remember looking around and know for sure
that I am living.
I am in the Land of the Living.

Something New

My bag is packed.
There is a thrill of something new.
Resolutions? No.
Just manifestations of wanting everything to be
brand new.
I've become the first responder of my life.
Resurrecting a body that's been beaten down and
can no longer live.
Those bags are packed.
It's time for something new.

The New Guy

Here comes the new guy.
Another one that I have to explain myself to.
There is no consistency.
No constant.
I sweat through each visit wondering what I'll
have to endure next.
Is there no freedom from judgment?
Is there no freedom from worry and wonder?
What next?
Dear God, what next?

Stained Glass

A calculated coloring book of primary stains and
hues.
This stained glass scripture has been the receiver
of many upturned views.
It is a river of azure water, embraced by emerald
green trees.
Where light beckons those who have sought her.
A Revelation wafting through the breeze.
I sit and wait for the restorative powers these
banks might bring to me.
Are they not made to cleanse and renew; these
waters of pale blue light?
I wait with my fellow travelers thirsting for the
healing powers of the River of Life.

The Reader

The books are left unread.
White noise rises from the pile.
This reader has fizzled out.
The words are dead.
There is no motivation in the imagination to
bring them back to life.
But you must resurrect them from their deathly
hallows.
You must live within the books.
There is more than just black and white between
the covers.
Your own story might get overlooked.

The Roses

They stand so tall, the roses there.
How grand they hold their heads.
The only glimpse of weakness are the ruddy
tears they shed.
Their legs are strong and stable now,
And their faces, like sweet red wine.
They seem to have no worry, that it will soon be
sleeping time.
Days and weeks have slipped on by,
And their heads are dark and bare.

Not a single blush of each glorious face is left
for them to share.
The snow begins to softly fall,
Laying down and feathers there.
The roses soon will slumber along the pathway
where glory once they shared.
They seem to never worry, the roses with heads
so bare.
I wonder is it their legs that whisper, "You really
should never fear."
Springtime comes with warmth and light, the
pathway so crisp with dew.
The roses, not quite awakened to see the lovely
view.
Their legs still strong and stalwart, the roses less
blackened and bruised.
Their faces have started to color with the pinkish
hue of rouge.
How long will they stay and visit me, these roses
along the path?
I often count the days until the petals appear
along the path,
And the weeping of the roses has once again
come back.

Last Good-byes

There's a parking spot that's empty.
No more rules define my day.
No key to unlock the door of stories,
And no more laughter echoing my way.
I closed the book of essays,
And locked the wooden door.
No more late night worries,
Leaving broken pencils lying on the floor.
The lights went out so easily on that cold and
bitter winter's day.
No more trying so hard that tears often fell,
No more childish games to play.
One last walk to my parking spot.
No more tears left in my eyes.
I drove out of that parking lot and said my last
good-byes.

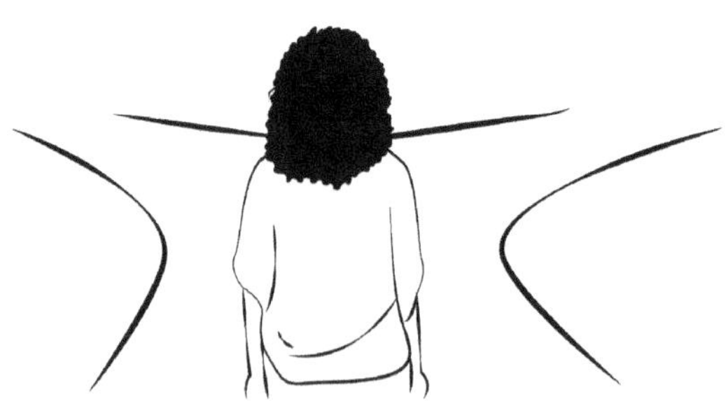

The Old Book

The cold brittle pages in a brown weathered
book,
Are protected from the elements and the
bitterness of the world.
The aged binding, broken from neverending use.
It lays dormant now,
Day after day waiting for a reminiscence of what
was written long ago.
Will it be loved again with a renewed purpose?
Or will it die and fade away with only dusty
cobwebs as their friend?

The Storm

The clouds gather and plunge light into the
darkness,
Abbreviating the day, sending it into the bleak
and early night.
Lightning flashes haphazardly and burns
whatever it touches.
Only the low rumble of thunder announces its
next flash and strike.
Trepidation and fear of the unknown stiffens the
body and breaks the soul.
Tremors jolt and tremble with the next
Flash! Bang! Crack!
The body is broken, sheared through like the
black burns left after the storm,
Never to heal, the scar reveals the havoc left by
the relentless storm.

Phoenix

I have been a witness to the fiery siege.
There is no way to turn the page.
It is a frozen heat so rare,
There is no explanation.
Like the ripping and tearing of pages from a
book—a novel never to be finished.
There are only beginnings that are rewritten over
and over again.

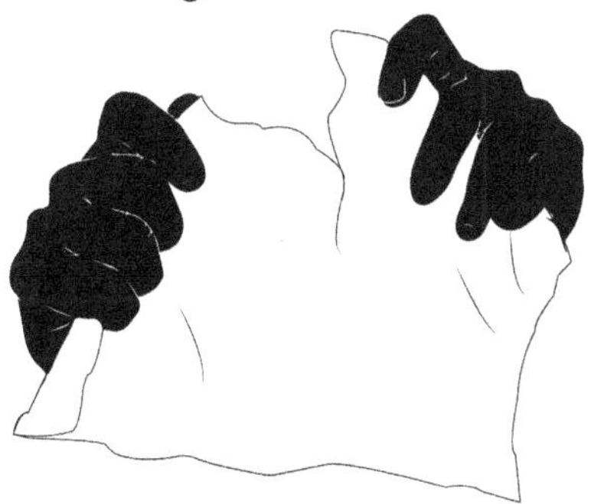

I sit now at the tabernacle of life, waiting for my
season.
Yet living each day like a phoenix:
Burning,
And then reborn only to burn again.
It is a never ending rewind.
Today, I read those same brittle pages with hope
in my heart,

Only to watch it combust in heat and fire once
again.
The monotony is exhausting.
There is no reprieve.
I wait for the ash, smoke and steam.
These are the only pardons I receive.
As the rising terror of being burned alive
consumes me.

A Sacred Place

Here I sit alone,
Watching fireflies dance and roam.
I am comforted by solace in this place,
Where words and thoughts are
invisible—erased.
My heart is unburdened and my soul adjusts.
There is privacy here, a sacred trust.
In this place I know I belong,
I wear no masks or disguises to look like I am
strong.

A Remedy in the Night

As deep winter's darkness blankets the land,
I seek solace within the cup in my hands.
A liquid embrace that makes me feel whole,
A mug of warm nectar, a remedy, for this weary
soul.
Its warmth seeps through every vein,
Chasing away the chill, dispelling my pain.
As I surrender to this nocturnal delight,
A symphony of flavor fills the stillness of night.
So, let the cold winds howl, and the night grow
long,
In its warmth, my dear companion, it is sweet
and strong.

Protected

47

There are endless reasons why some things
shatter and burn the exterior.
I'm never sure why the fire always knows where
to singe and scar.
But one thing that is always protected is the
beating heart, behind the door with rusty hinges.

Warrior

In a world of make believe and fanciful dreams,
I navigate a path that can't be seen.
Guided only by stars at night,
Memories dance in a playground of delight.
But lurking in the shadows with venomous
intent,
A bully waits to leave me broken, scarred and
spent.
Yet seeds of resilience were sown.
They taught me strength and that I'm never
alone.
So let the battles I've fought blossom within me
as a fearless warrior, strong and free.

Sit Beside Me

Come, sit down in this chair beside me.
You've been watching shadows far too long.
The distorted sounds of rage have consumed
your mind from hearing sweet and lovely songs.
A lyric of hope and good fortune that will come
from an unexpected call.
A revelation awaits to embrace you before you
take that private fall.

Guarded Warning

Dear Companion,
        I'm delighted by the final drops of the
falling rain.
I witnessed your unfolding of beauty
unrestrained.
You must be very careful, though, for whispers
still remain.
That although your radiance will sustain, the
internal scars will cause you inoperable pain.

A Path to Follow

In shattered lands, where chaos brews,
A wooden leg strides, defying the blues.
It is a testament to the human will,
To rise above, and conquer still.

Though the world may crumble,
And tremors shake,
Hope remains steadfast,
Refusing to break.
For in the face of nature's wrath,
We find the strength to follow a new path.

Useless

I heard the murmurs and rumors of those who
walked back into the shadows.
They placed a lid over the unfortunate saying,
"Call me when it's over."
The shell was broken.
No pearl could grow inside.
"Leave it there."
"Let it die."
That's what happens when you're no use to
them.
Worthless.
Hopeless.
Forgotten.

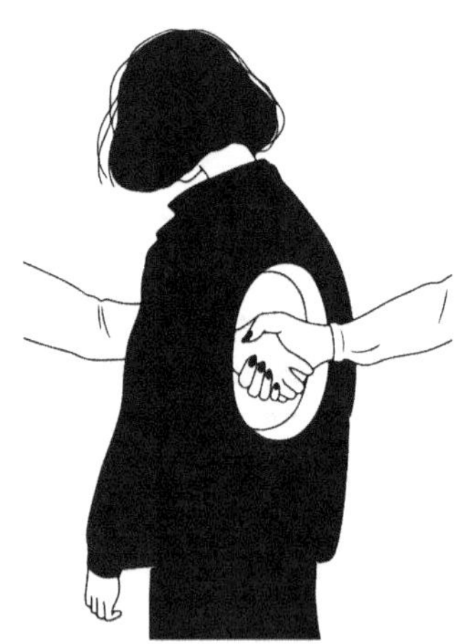

Live Each Day

An opalescent colored blanket crystalized in my
mind.
It evoked a stillness and peace, that as of late, I
have yet to find.
Is it a memory from the past;
Something I've forgotten in my haste?
Or is it a glimpse of angel's wings, reminding
me that time, I truly should not waste.

These words I often live by as I awake to the
morning rays.
I know that Father Time and his ticking clock
have given me another day.

It's a Mystery

I was going to write a fairy tale that started with,
"Once Upon a Time…"
But when I thought of writing the ending it
struck me that this was a novel with a twisted
plot line.
The story kept me asking, How and Why?
Now I realize there are no answers to end this
timeline.
There was an alchemy of characters and villains
that dithered along wayward paths.
How do you write a story when even the narrator
gets lost and circles back.
A person can only read and reread a story on
repeat before they close the book.
I'm not even sure there's a final destination or a
death defying hook.
For now this crazy story has only one mood,
     "To Be Continued"

Chapter Two

Fast Forward…
To a new dream.
The old one in a file…
A smile and a good-bye.
There is merit in the life I've lived…
No regrets…
Only pride in the challenges and perseverance.
Despite the pain and struggle and doubt…
The loss of a life loved.
My tomorrows are filled…
New challenges…
A new love of life.
Chapter two is new…
I dream of a life to be loved…
No pain…
No sorrow…
Only joy and anticipation for the next tomorrow.

Grieving

I dwelled on a talent that slipped away.
A grief laid bare with a deluge of hot, wet tears.
A human reaction to death, no?
I looked out my window and felt the emptiness,
A paralyzing dread of loneliness and fear.
This rush of fire has enveloped my entire being,
Anger and pain are so consuming.
I felt the ringing in my ears like a hot
hallucinating fever.
I dwelled on talent that slipped away,
But there are no more tears,

An arid lens stares intently toward the future.
A human reaction to acceptance, no?
The stubbornness and will to pry open the
windows and breathe in a new day.

I Am Alive

I am not dead. I am alive.
Life, much like poetry, has potential from the
beginning to the end.
A haphazardly, and sometimes speedy, motion of
experiences looping through concentric and
overlapping circles of time.
New beginnings throughout each circle expand
and balloon aimlessly until Father Time steps in
and offers another chance.
But when is enough, just enough?
Does the mind or the body decide?
Is the choice even mine?
Today, it doesn't matter.
I am alive. I am not dead.
The potential for the next verse still lives in me.

www.ingramcontent.com/pod-product-compliance
Lightning Source LLC
LaVergne TN
LVHW050932200726
843508LV00011B/2324